Pocket

Magna Carta

1217 Text and Translation

Bodleian Library
UNIVERSITY OF OXFORD

First published in 2016 by the Bodleian Library
Broad Street, Oxford OX1 3BG
www.bodleianshop.co.uk
2nd impression 2019
3rd impression 2022
4th impression 2025

ISBN: 978 1 85124 452 2

Designed by Dot Little at the Bodleian Library
Typeset by JCS Publishing Services Ltd in 10pt on 12pt Minion Pro
Printed and bound in Slovenia by DZS Grafik on 100gsm Munken Print Cream paper

FSC www.fsc.org MIX Paper | Supporting responsible forestry FSC® C106600

British Library Catalogue in Publishing Data
A CIP record of this publication is available from the British Library

CONTENTS

INTRODUCTION

Magna Carta, the Great Charter, is arguably the single most important legal document ever created. From its origins as a peace treaty between a medieval king and his rebellious subjects, it has become widely regarded today as the embodiment of the ideal of individual protection under the law, guaranteeing freedom from the fear of imprisonment without due process of the law as well as the right to a fair and free trial. These twin pillars underpin the justice systems of many states worldwide. Throughout its 800-year history, Magna Carta has been referenced again and again as a touchstone of democratic liberties. It can be regarded as the forerunner to the Founding Documents of the United States of America, to the Declaration of the Rights of Man approved by the National Assembly of France in 1789, and to the key articles in the Universal Declaration of Human Rights, published in 1948 by the United Nations. Today, it possesses a totemic status as a bulwark against tyrannical rule, embodying the very ideals of justice and liberty and the expression of these concepts in many forms.

Origins

Magna Carta originated in 1215 essentially as a peace treaty between King John (*r.* 1199–1216) and his rebellious subjects – barons, bishops and freemen – who combined to challenge him near the end of his disastrous reign. In England, his governance had been a story of greed, cruelty and incompetence. Abroad, he had lost most of his predecessors' lands in France and wasted England's wealth in failed campaigns to recover them. He had quarrelled so severely with the pope over Church questions that he and his court were excommunicated and the English Church forbidden under an Interdict from performing its functions. In 1215, matters came to a head with the rebels' seizure of London, forcing John into negotiations which culminated on 15 June at Runnymede, a meadow between Windsor and Staines close to the river Thames. There John assented to a charter of liberties.

The archbishop of Canterbury, Stephen Langton, is said to have discovered precedents for the control of royal power in the charters of liberties granted and guaranteed by John's predecessors, Henry I, Stephen and Henry II at their coronations – in particular, Henry I's coronation charter of 1100. However, whilst Henry I's charter comprised no more than fourteen clauses, that agreed by King John in 1215 had as many as sixty-three.

In addition to clauses enshrining due legal process and a fair trial, the Magna Carta of 1215 placed further limits on the king's powers. 'No scutage or aid [in effect no taxation] is to be imposed in our realm except by the common counsel of our realm.' (From the germ of this concept arose the demand of the leaders of the American Revolution for 'No Taxation without Representation'.) This counsel could only be achieved by a meeting – that is, a council – of the designated men of the realm, summoned in accordance with agreed procedures. Magna Carta's requirement in 1215 that the king seek the counsel of the realm – although almost eliminated in later reissues – can be regarded as the origin of an official body later known as Parliament, which in the span of forty years from the sealing of the Great Charter was capable of meeting without the presence of the king.

The official document evidently sealed by John at Runnymede on 15 June 1215 has not survived. A document with John's seal now at the British Library in London, known as 'The Articles of the Barons', appears to be a draft set of proposals. Official copies (or engrossments) of the finalized text of Magna Carta, issued by the king's chancery, were sent out a few weeks later in 1215, effectively to the English counties but perhaps initially at the instigation of bishops for preservation at their cathedrals; four examples of 1215 now survive: two at the British Library, one at Lincoln Cathedral and one at Salisbury Cathedral. The medieval home of one of the British Library examples has recently been identified as Canterbury Cathedral, although the copy itself is now almost entirely illegible. These original medieval locations illustrate how the Great Charter was distributed throughout the realm.

Survival of Magna Carta

King John himself had no intention of honouring a document which aimed to subordinate him to his subjects by creating a committee of twenty-five barons to enforce the Charter against any potential royal misdeeds. A copy was sent to Rome; and within just twelve weeks of the issue of the 1215 Magna Carta, Pope Innocent III annulled the document on 24 August 1215. At home, King John ignored the provisions of the Charter, placing himself again at loggerheads with the barons. By September, the country was once more plunged into conflict and the Runnymede peace settlement was dead. Civil war ensued. Prince Louis of France (later Louis VIII) invaded England, ruling over large swathes of the south of the country.

Effectively terminated, Magna Carta would thus have died a quiet death, had not King John himself perished only sixteen months after affixing his seal to the Great Charter. After his death on 18/19 October 1216, his nine-year-old son succeeded as King Henry III. His guardians, the papal legate Cardinal Guala Bicchieri of Vercelli and the Earl of Pembroke, William Marshal, had him crowned only a few days later at Gloucester Abbey. By way of an apology for previous royal misdeeds and as a pledge of good government to come, they sent out the boy king's first reissue of Magna Carta, over his name but with their own seals, from Bristol in November 1216.

This version had only forty-two clauses, omitting those of 1215 which had most strongly limited the king's powers: e.g. the clauses referring to the 'common counsel of our realm' – implying the establishment of a proto-parliament of bishops and barons – and the closing clause establishing a group of twenty-five barons to enforce Magna Carta even over the king. Other omitted clauses of 1215 had covered money-lending, for example, with a reference to the Jews, and more immediate matters such as the return of hostages held by the king, including those from Wales and Scotland, a call for all foreign knights and mercenaries to leave the realm, and a pardon for those who had rebelled against the king. The 1216 issue ends with a summary of the omitted clauses, saying that these 'weighty and doubtful' subjects were to be left aside for the time being for more considered debate.

Henry III's second issue of Magna Carta, issued only a year later in November 1217, lacks 1216's concluding admission of provisionality and may therefore be taken as the more final statement promised there. At forty-seven clauses, it contains five more clauses than 1216. Some of the new clauses govern the holding of local courts (Clauses 15 and 42), or more detailed issues such as Clause 26, 'No estate cart of any ecclesiastical person or knight or any lady may be taken by ... bailiffs.' The final Clause 47, requiring the demolition of unauthorized ('adulterine') castles built during the rebellion against King John, appears unique to 1217 and is its only clause to mention Henry's father. This clause also includes 1217's only reference to the 'common counsel of our kingdom' – still spelt '*consilium*' (counsel), not '*concilium*' (council) – which had been mentioned more often in the now-deleted clauses of 1215.

By 1217, such was the status of Magna Carta that it was already being referred to as the 'big' or 'great' (*magna*) charter to differentiate it from a new, lesser charter which governed the king's control over the forests, known as the 'Charter of the Forest'. This shorter charter re-established rights of access and use for freemen in the royal forests. Two originals of the 1217 Forest Charter now survive, at Lincoln and Durham.

Henry III reissued Magna Carta in 1225 as an attempt to negotiate taxation between the Church and the Crown. This document, sealed with his own Great Seal now that he was about to come of age, is redivided into only thirty-seven clauses. The 1225 version and its confirmation in 1297 by Henry's son King Edward I (in the same thirty-seven clauses) were the versions by which Magna Carta after its various modifications entered English law.

Most of Magna Carta's clauses were repealed by Parliament in the nineteenth century. Today, just a few clauses are still in force under English law. They survived and were transmitted, albeit with differing clause-numbers, through the various issues from 1215 onwards. They are taken in this instance from the issue of 1217:

Clause 1

First, we have granted to God and by this our present charter have confirmed on behalf of us and our heirs for ever, that the English church is to be free and is to have her rights in full and her liberties unharmed. We have also granted to all the freemen of our kingdom, on behalf of us and our heirs for ever, all the underwritten liberties to be held by them and by their heirs from us and from our heirs.

Clause 10

The City of London is to have all its ancient liberties and its free customs. Furthermore, we desire and grant that all other cities and boroughs and settlements and the Barons of the Cinque Ports [*five ports on the south-east coast of England*] and all ports may have all liberties and their free customs.

Clauses 35–6

35. No freeman is to be taken or imprisoned, or dispossessed of his free tenement or liberties or his free customs, or be outlawed or exiled, or in any other way destroyed, nor will we go against him, nor send against him, except through the lawful judgment of his peers or through the law of the land.

36. To no one shall we sell, to no one shall we deny or delay right or justice.

Influence of Magna Carta

Magna Carta survived in England in another, perhaps more important, way than is implied by these clauses. From Tudor times onwards, the document began to be studied by historians and jurists, and to be invoked as an ideal, accurately or inaccurately, by both reformers and reactionaries, rather than for its specific policies.

The invention of printing in the mid-fifteenth century made possible the wider distribution of the Great Charter. As early as 1481, the first abridgement of English statutes was printed by John Lettou and William De Machlinia in their *Abbreviamentum Statutorum*. Created as a handbook for lawyers, the book summarizes and categorizes English law. Under the section entitled 'Peers of the Kingdom' is a summary of the crucial clause of the 1225 issue of Magna Carta, forbidding imprisonment and punishment of a freeman without due process of the law and judgment of his peers.

The first printing of Magna Carta in full (in Latin) was undertaken by Richard Pynson (the king's printer) in 1508, in a volume which contains the 1225 issue together with a number of other 'Ancient Statutes'. The book was immensely popular, appearing in at least twenty editions by the end of the sixteenth century and inspiring the compilation of similar collections of legal texts by competing printers. The first edition of Magna Carta in English was produced in 1534 by George Ferrers in his *Boke of Magna Carta*, which reproduced all thirty-seven clauses of the 1225 issue – though with significant errors by both the translator and the typesetter.

While these books were produced largely for the legal book trade, they nevertheless directly influenced popular thinking about Magna Carta and contributed to its status as a document with considerable legal significance. From the early sixteenth century onwards, Magna Carta was cited in legal cases as a means of preventing royal attempts to interfere in the due legal process. Within just two years of Ferrers' English translation, the clause guaranteeing the freedom of the English Church was used by those who opposed Henry VIII's religious reforms, including Sir Thomas More (1478–1535), who referenced Magna Carta at his trial in 1535.

In the late sixteenth and early seventeenth centuries, legal scholars such as Sir Edward Coke (1552–1634) and John Selden (1584–1654) interpreted Magna Carta as a confirmation of the principle of individual liberty existing in England from very early times. While other statutes could be legally repealed, Magna Carta was irrevocable, because it was seen as preserving original liberties granted to the English people against the power of kings. This interpretation was based in part on a misreading of the phrase '*liber homo*', which signified in the thirteenth century a precise category of privileged 'freeman' but was later translated more generally as meaning any 'free man', or indeed everyone. However, this distinction was not properly understood until much later, and in the conflict which pitted Charles I (*r.* 1625–49) against the House of Commons, the bitter argument of individual liberties versus royal powers and prerogative resulted in legal conflicts and a constitutional challenge to the Crown, culminating in the Civil

War and the execution of Charles I. While the monarchy was restored in 1660, the place of Magna Carta as a charter of individual freedoms became a lasting reality with considerable political impact. It is therefore Magna Carta's general reputation and influence, as an ideal for the rule of law and constitutional government, which are of far greater importance than any lingering survival of individual clauses.

Up until the mid-eighteenth century, the version of Magna Carta which had the widest currency was the issue of 1225. William Blackstone (1723–1780), a judge, politician and professor in the University of Oxford, published the first modern critical edition of Magna Carta (1759), distinguishing for the first time between the several surviving versions issued between 1215 and 1297. Blackstone is responsible for numbering each of the clauses of Magna Carta, which differ from version to version, and his system is still in use today. His commentary on Magna Carta, contained in his great work *Commentaries on the Laws of England* (1765–9), had the effect of placing Magna Carta in even greater esteem and generally increasing its reputation. Like his predecessors, Blackstone erroneously presented Magna Carta not as the product of a settlement between King John and the barons but as an 'Ancient Constitution', stretching back into the very mists of time.

Magna Carta and North America

Blackstone's work on Magna Carta, like those of his legal antecedents such as Sir Edward Coke, was studied in the American colonies. Since England was by nature a land of liberty, it was evident that the colonies should also enjoy the same liberties as Englishmen at home. This idea became formalized in the charters offered by Charles I to his colonies of Massachusetts (1629), Maryland (1632), Maine (1639) and others. During the English Civil War, the liberties which were seen as flowing from Magna Carta were held as a form of protection by Parliament against royal powers. However, in the course of the eighteenth century it was Parliament which came to be seen as the oppressor of the American colonies, chiefly by a cycle of unpopular Parliamentary acts, including the Sugar Act (1764), the Stamp Act (1765), the Declaratory Act (1766), the Townshend Acts (1767) and the Coercive Acts (1774).

This did not stop Magna Carta from being seen as a potent weapon by the American colonists in their struggle against their English rulers. By recasting the Great Charter as an agreement between the King and the people (in which all mention of Parliament was expunged), they enlisted Magna Carta in the struggle against King George III for individual liberties which he had violated. On the eve of the American Revolution, Paul Revere was commissioned to redraw the seal of Massachusetts, which now depicted a patriot holding in one hand a drawn sword and brandishing in the other a copy of Magna Carta.

Thus in 1776, the architects of the Declaration of Independence recognized in Magna Carta a precedent for expressing their grievances against George III. Magna Carta entered more directly into the legal framework of the newly established United States in the form of paraphrases of those clauses which address due legal process, and eventually into the Bill of Rights (1791). For example, the Fifth Amendment guarantees that 'No person shall … be deprived of life, liberty, or property, without due process of law.' In addition, the text of Magna Carta found its way directly into the statute books of no fewer than seventeen states, most recently in North Dakota in 1943. Ironically therefore, Magna Carta survives to a greater extent in American than in British law.

Today, Magna Carta retains its totemic status, encompassing concepts of justice and liberty and as the embodiment of the spirit of freedom. It is frequently cited as a guarantor of individual rights and as a benchmark for the rule of law, higher than any king or ruler.

The surviving documents

The chancery scribes of a medieval English king worked as a small élite team at the sovereign's court, usually travelling with him but otherwise based at Westminster. Their business was both to transmit and to record the decisions of the sovereign, and thereby to maintain the official records of the state and of legal decisions. For the writs which they sent out as well as for state records, they used a standard and distinctive style of writing, known as chancery script. They were also influential in the use, development and standardization of official languages, in Latin, French and (from the fifteenth century) English. Recent research suggests that, for the multiple official duplicates needed to promulgate Magna Carta, bishops lent their own scribes to help the chancery team.

All in all, Magna Carta was issued perhaps up to a dozen times in the thirteenth century, the last issue promulgated by Edward I in 1300. What lay behind all these reissues is that Magna Carta contained highly expedient principles which could be used for negotiations between the sovereign and his Church or government whenever problems arose. Of these, originals of the issues of 1215, 1216, 1217, 1225, 1297 and 1300 survive, with later copies of the issue of 1265. Of the twenty-four surviving originals of Magna Carta issued in the thirteenth century up to 1300, five are preserved at the Bodleian Library in Oxford. These include three of the 1217 issue, and one each of 1225 and 1300. It is the issue of 1217 as later preserved at Gloucester Abbey which is transcribed and translated in this book.

The seals affixed to this charter confirm its status as an original issued in 1217 by the royal chancery. Its destination as the official copy sent to the county of Gloucestershire in south-west England is indicated by the two medieval endorsements written on its back. These are recognizable by comparison with other documents as the archival markings of the Benedictine Abbey of St Peter, Gloucester.

St Peter's had been the city's dominant religious community from Anglo-Saxon and Norman times. After its dissolution as a monastery by Henry VIII in 1540 it was refounded as Gloucester Cathedral in 1541, and under that name its medieval church and magnificent fan-vaulted cloister stand proud to this day. St Peter's was said to have found favour with Henry VIII since its church contained the tomb of his predecessor King Edward II (*d.* 1327), the grandson of Henry III who had reissued this Magna Carta as a boy in 1217.

The exact date and circumstances of this Magna Carta leaving Gloucester Abbey or Cathedral archives are unknown, but it is found next in the hands of Rev. Richard Furney (1694–1753), a native of Gloucester.

Furney was master of the city's Crypt School (now a grammar school) from 1719 to 1724, a scholar of local history and a collector of documents and antiquities. In 1720 he had been employed by the city corporation to reorganize its archives. He was a graduate of Oriel College, Oxford (BA 1715, MA 1718), and a friend of one of the Bodleian's great scholar-librarians, Thomas Hearne. Later he became archdeacon of Surrey (1725–53) and bequeathed to the Bodleian Library six manuscripts relating to Gloucestershire and eighteen 'ancient deeds and charters'. These included this original Magna Carta of 1217 and two later originals (the subsidiary 'Parva Carta' issued by Henry III in 1237 and the reissue of 1301 with the Great Seal of Edward I). Furney's bequest reached Oxford in 1755, two years after his death.

A palaeographical and diplomatic account of the Gloucester Charter

The Latin text of this 1217 Magna Carta (Oxford, Bodleian Library, MS. Ch. Glouc. 8) was written with many abbreviations (as standard in medieval writing, to save space) by one scribe in fifty-six long lines. While the handwriting is parallel to the more formal gothic style of manuscript books, it is specifically a 'chancery script', here written rather quickly and cursively with a backwards slant, but tending towards extension and flourish. In the top line, the king's name 'Henricus' starts with a decorative 'H' and ends with an exaggerated long 's', and the scribe uses the upper margin to stretch the initials and ascending pen-strokes of Henry's further titles and the list of his addressees.

On the right, in dark green wax, the small round equestrian seal (*c.* 35 mm diameter) showing William Marshal on horseback survives almost perfectly, though the design is somewhat blurred. On the left, in white wax, the design of Cardinal Guala's oval seal (*c.* 40 x 30 mm) is now completely lost and the lump of wax apparently reversed to show its original rounded back. However, the engraving of this charter's seals published in William Blackstone's edition of 1759 shows part of Guala's design still surviving, albeit already fragmentary, with the central part of the cardinal's torso in his ecclesiastical robes and some of the lettering on either side.

Materials used in making Magna Carta

The ink of MS. Ch. Glouc. 8 is dark brown, occasionally abraded but not powdering, so probably an iron-gall ink rather than the blacker carbon-based type. The scribe would have used a quill pen, probably a goose quill, cut to a chisel-edged point. The parchment is from a single skin, cut not quite straight, between 529 and 541 mm in height (as folded, discounting the seals) by 418 to 436 mm in width. The text is written on the skin's flesh side, now greyish in tone. The hair side, the back of the document, is yellower and more mottled, suggesting that, despite its large size, the parchment may be sheepskin or even goatskin rather than calfskin. The wax of each seal surrounds two thin parchment tags which are attached through single slits at the charter's foot, where the parchment is folded over twice to receive them – the standard method using a double tag known in medieval French as *sur double queue*. Later creases show that for storage the whole skin was folded five times over as a tight packet, enclosing its seals, to a thirty-second of its unfolded size. Endorsements briefly describing the contents were added on the outside of the folded packet from medieval times and up to the eighteenth century.

BCBB & SF

A note on the text

The original Latin text is heavily abbreviated. In the Latin transcription printed here, nearly all of these abbreviations have been silently expanded. Pointed brackets are used in the Latin to mark expansions of a few unclear abbrev<iations> and to supply <omitted words>, and more frequently in the translation to supply additional <clarifying> words. Square brackets and italics are used in both texts to mark [*editorial comments*].

TRANSLATION

THE GREAT CHARTER

[November 1217]

(Oxford, Bodleian Library, MS. Ch. Glouc. 8)

Henry by the grace of God king of England, lord of Ireland, duke of Normandy and Aquitaine, and earl of Anjou, to the archbishops, bishops, abbots, priors, earls, barons, sheriffs, governors, officers and all bailiffs and his faithful subjects, about to inspect this present charter – Greeting. Know ye that, in respect for God and for the salvation of our soul and the souls of our ancestors and successors, to the exaltation of Holy Church and the improvement of our kingdom, we have granted and by this present charter have confirmed for us and for our heirs for ever, by the counsel of our venerable father the lord Gualo, cardinal priest of the title of St Martin and legate of the apostolic see, the lord Walter archbishop of York, William bishop of London and other bishops of England, and William Marshal earl of Pembroke, guardian of us and of our kingdom, and our other faithful earls and barons of England, these underwritten liberties, to be held in our kingdom of England for ever.

1. First, we have granted to God and by this our present charter have confirmed on behalf of us and our heirs for ever, that the English church is to be free and is to have her rights in full and her liberties unharmed. We have also granted to all the freemen of our kingdom, on behalf of us and our heirs for ever, all the underwritten liberties to be held by them and by their heirs from us and from our heirs.

2. If any of our earls or barons or our other tenants in chief through military service [*holding lands directly from the king*] shall have died, and at his death his heir shall have been of full age and may owe a relief [*inheritance fee*], the heir may possess his inheritance through the ancient relief: that is, the heir or heirs of an earl, an earl's barony whole for one hundred pounds: the heir or heirs of a baron, a barony whole for one hundred pounds: the heir or heirs of a knight, a knight's fee-holding whole for one hundred shillings at most; and he who shall have owed less may give less, according to the ancient custom of fees.

3. If however the heir of any such persons shall have been under age, his lord is not to have the wardship of him or his land before receiving his homage; and after such an heir shall have been in ward, when he shall have come of age, that is twenty-one years, he may have his inheritance without relief and without fine; so that, however, even if he shall have been made a knight <whilst> under age, his land is nevertheless to remain in the wardship of his lords up to the term aforesaid.

4. The warden of the land of such an under-age heir is not to take from the heir's land any but reasonable proceeds and reasonable customs and reasonable services, and this without destruction and waste of men or goods. And if we shall have committed the custody of any land of any such heir to a sheriff, or to any other person who ought to answer to us for the proceeds of that land, and he shall have caused destruction or waste of his wardship, we shall recover damages from him, and the land is to be committed to two lawful and discreet men of the same fee-holding, who are to answer for the proceeds to us or to him to whom we shall have assigned them. And if we shall have given or sold to anyone the wardship of any such land, and he shall then have made destruction or waste upon it, let him lose the wardship, and let it be handed over to two lawful and discreet men of the same fee-holding, who are to answer to us in the same way as said above.

5. The warden however, as long as he shall have had wardship of the land, is to maintain the houses, parks, warrens, ponds, mills and other things belonging to that land, out of the proceeds of the same land, and is to hand back to the heir, when he shall have reached full age, his whole estate, restored with ploughs and all other things, at least in as far as he received it. All these things are to be observed in the wardships of vacant archbishoprics, bishoprics, abbeys, priories, churches and dignities, which appertain to us, except that wardships of this type ought not to be sold.

6. Heirs are to be married without disparagement [*dishonour to a woman resulting from marriage to a man of inferior rank*].

7. A widow, after the death of her husband, is to have immediately and without any difficulty her marriage portion [*land assigned for her upkeep before her husband's death*] and her inheritance; nor is she to give anything for her dower [*land assigned for her use after her husband's death*] and for her marriage portion, or for her inheritance which her husband and she shall have held on the day of his death; and she is to remain in the principal messuage [*dwelling house and lands*] of her husband for forty days after her husband's death, within which time her dower is to be assigned to her, unless it shall have been assigned to her before, or unless that house is a castle; and if she shall have departed from the castle, let there at once be provided for her a suitable house in which she may decently dwell, until her dower may be assigned to her as said above. And she is to have her reasonable estovers of the common [*necessaries for maintenance*]. And for her dower, let there be assigned to her the third part of all the land of her husband which was his in his lifetime, unless she shall have been dowered with less at the church door [*at her marriage ceremony*].

8. No widow may be distrained [*legally forced*] to get married while she shall have wished to live without a husband; but yet she is to give security that she will not get married without our assent if she shall have held <land> from us, or without the assent of her lord if she shall have held from another.

9. We indeed or our bailiffs will not seize any land or rent for any debt, as long as the present chattels of the debtor are sufficient for paying the debt, and the debtor himself may be prepared to make satisfaction of it; nor may the guarantors of the debtor himself be distrained, as long as the principal debtor himself may be good for the payment of the debt. And if the principal debtor shall have failed in payment of the debt, not having the wherewithal to discharge it, or is unwilling to discharge it when he could, the guarantors are to answer for the debt; and if they wish, let them have the lands and rents of the debtor until satisfaction be made to them for the debt which they shall have paid for him before, unless the principal debtor shall have shown himself acquitted of it against the same guarantors.

10. The City of London is to have all its ancient liberties and its free customs. Furthermore, we desire and grant that all other cities and boroughs and settlements and the Barons of the Cinque Ports [*five ports on the south-east coast of England*] and all ports may have all liberties and their free customs.

11. No one is to be distrained to do more service for a knight's fee-holding, nor for any other free tenement, than what is due from it.

12. Common Pleas [*civil actions at law*] are not to follow our court <on its travels>, but shall be held in some fixed place.

13. Trials of Novel Disseisin [*to recover seized property*] <and> of Mort d'Ancestor [*to recover an* *inheritance*] are not to be held except in their own counties, and in this manner: we, or our Chief Justiciary if we shall have been outside the kingdom, will send justiciaries throughout every county once in the year, who with the knights of the counties are to hold in the counties the aforesaid assizes.

14. And those matters, which at that arrival in the county cannot be determined by the aforesaid justiciaries sent to take the said assizes, are to be determined by them elsewhere in their circuit; and those matters which cannot be determined by them, because of the difficulty of some articles, are to be referred to our Justiciaries of the Bench [*royal judges sitting at Westminster*] and there determined.

15. Assizes of Last Presentation [*cases concerning church patronage or benefices*] are always to be taken before our Justiciaries of the Bench and there determined.

16. A freeman is not to be amerced [*fined or punished at a court's discretion*] for a small offence except according to the measure of that offence; and for a great offence according to the magnitude of the offence, saving his contenement [*i.e. without threatening his freeholding or maybe other qualifying property*]; and a merchant in the same manner, saving his merchandise; and a serf belonging to another rather than ours is to be amerced in the same manner, saving his wainage [*means of livelihood, or agricultural tools?*], if he shall have fallen at our mercy; and none of the aforesaid amercements is to be imposed except through the oaths of honest and lawful men of the neighbourhood.

17. Earls and barons are not to be amerced except through their peers and not except according to the measure of their offence.

18. No ecclesiastical person is to be amerced according to the greatness of his ecclesiastical benefice, but only according to his lay-fee [*land held in return for secular services*], and according to the greatness of his offence.

19. Neither a settlement nor a man is to be distrained to build bridges at [*for* or?] embankments, except those who of old and of right ought to do it.

20. No embankment is henceforth to be defended, except those which were in defence in the time of King Henry our grandfather [*Henry II*] throughout the same places and the same boundaries as they were accustomed to be in his time.

21. No sheriff, constable, coroners or other bailiffs of ours are to hold Pleas of our Crown [*legal proceedings in which the Crown had a financial interest*].

22. If anyone holding a lay fee from us should die, and the sheriff or our bailiff should show our Letters Patent of our summons [*royal authorization*] concerning a debt which the dead man owed to us, let it be lawful for the sheriff or our bailiff to seize and register the chattels of the dead man found on the lay fee, to the value of that debt in the view of lawful men; so that, nothing may be removed from there until the debt be paid to us clear, and the rest is to be left to the executors to fulfil the Will of the dead man; and if nothing may be owing to us by him, all the chattels are to fall to the <Will of the> dead man, saving to his wife her reasonable shares [*sons here omitted*].

23. No constable or his bailiff is to take the corn or other goods of anyone who may not be of that settlement where the castle is situated, unless he at once pay money for them or can have respite by the free will of the seller; but if he shall have been of the settlement itself, let the price be rendered within forty days.

24. No constable shall distrain any knight into giving him money for castle guard, if he himself shall have been willing to perform it in his own person, or through another able man if he could not perform it himself for a reasonable cause; and if we shall have led or sent him into the army, he shall be excused from guard duty, according to the extent of time that he shall have been with us in the army, on account of the fee for which he has done service in the army.

25. No sheriff or bailiff of ours or another's may take the horses or carts of anyone for the purpose of carriage, unless he hands over the payment established of old: that is, for a cart with two horses, ten pence per day, and for a cart with three horses, fourteen pence per day.

26. No estate cart of any ecclesiastical person or knight or any lady may be taken by the aforesaid bailiffs.

27. Neither we nor our own bailiffs nor another's shall take another man's wood, for castles or for conducting other business of ours, except by consent of him whose wood that shall have been.

28. We shall not hold the lands of those who have been convicted of felony except for one year and one day, and then the lands are to be returned to the lords of the fees.

29. All fish weirs henceforth are to be entirely removed along the Thames or <the River> Medway, and throughout all England except the sea coast.

30. The writ which is called 'Praecipe' [*a writ of covenant, issued in a dispute over a land agreement*] is henceforth not to be granted to anyone in respect of any tenement, whereby a freeman may lose his <right to access> court.

31. Let there be one measure for wine throughout our whole kingdom, and one measure for ale, and one measure for corn, namely the quarter<-measure> of London; and one breadth for dyed cloths, russets and haubergets [*types of cloth*], namely, two ells within the cloth-borders. For weights, indeed, it is to be the same as with measures.

32. Nothing is to be given henceforth for a writ of inquest by him who seeks an inquest of life or limbs; but let it be conceded without charge, and not denied.

33. If anyone may hold from us through fee-farm or socage or through burgage [*forms of land-tenure held through various modes of rent or service*], and may hold land from another through knight service, we will not have wardship of the heir, nor of his land which is of another's fee, on account of that fee-farm or socage or burgage; nor will we have wardship of that fee-farm or socage or burgage, unless the fee-farm itself may owe knight service. We will not have the custody of the heir, nor of anyone's land which he holds from another through knight service, on account of any petty serjeanty [*small tenure*] which he holds of us through the service of rendering daggers or arrows or the like.

34. No bailiff henceforth may put anyone to his open law [*bring him to trial*], nor to an oath upon his own plain word, without faithful witnesses produced for that purpose.

35. No freeman is to be taken or imprisoned, or dispossessed of his free tenement or liberties or his free customs, or be outlawed or exiled, or in any other way destroyed, nor will we go against him, nor send against him, except through the lawful judgment of his peers or through the law of the land.

36. To no one shall we sell, to no one shall we deny or delay right or justice.

37. All merchants, unless publicly prohibited beforehand, are to have safe and secure conduct to go out of England and to come into England, and to stay and to go throughout England, as much by land as by water, for buying or for selling free of all evil tolls, according to ancient and right customs, except in time of war. And if they be from a land at war against us, and if such <merchants> may be found in our land at the beginning of the war, they are to be apprehended without injury to their bodies or goods, until it be known by us or by our Chief Justiciary how the merchants of our own land who may then be found in the land at war against us may be treated; and if ours be safe there, let the others be safe in our land.

38. If any shall have held from any escheat [*land lapsed by reversion to its feudal overlord after the tenant's death*], such as from the honour of Wallingford, Boulogne, Nottingham, Lancaster or from other escheats which are in our hand and which may be baronies, and shall have died, his heir is not to give other relief nor do for us any other service, than he would do for the baron if that <escheat> had been in the hand of the baron; and we shall hold it in the same manner that the baron held it. Nor shall we, by occasion of such a barony or escheat, have any escheat or the wardship of any of our men, unless he who held the barony or escheat shall have held elsewhere from us in chief [*directly from the king*].

39. No freeman henceforth is to give to anyone or sell any more of his own land than may, from the residue of his land, be sufficient to enable the lord of the fee to obtain the service due him which belongs to that fee.

40. All abbey patrons, who hold charters of the kings of England by advowson [*right of ecclesiastical patronage*] or who hold ancient tenure or possession, are to have custody of the abbeys when vacant, as they ought to have and as it has been declared above.

41. No one is to be apprehended or imprisoned on the appeal of a woman for the death of any man other than her own husband.

42. No county court henceforth may be held except from month to month; and where a greater term used to be, let it be the greater. Nor may any sheriff or his bailiff make his tourn through the hundred [*a court visit through a county division*] except twice in the year, and not except in the due and accustomed place, that is to say, once after Easter and again after the Feast of Saint Michael [29 *September*]. And the view of frank-pledge [*court or investigation of householders' mutual responsibilities*] is then to be taken at that term of St Michael, without exception, that is to say so that every man may have his liberties, which he had and used to have in the time of King Henry our grandfather, or which he acquired afterwards. Indeed the view of frank-pledge is to be taken thus, namely that our peace is to be kept, and that the tithing [*group of ten householders*] is to be kept complete as it thus used to be, and that the sheriff is not to seek exceptions, and that he is to be content with that which the sheriff used to have from taking his view in the time of King Henry our grandfather.

43. Let it not be lawful for anyone henceforth to give his land to any religious house, so that he may take it back as a holding from the same house. Nor let it be lawful for any religious house to accept the land of anyone, so as to hand it back as a holding to him from whom it shall have been received. But if anyone henceforth shall thus have given his land to any religious house, and be convicted of this, let his gift be utterly voided and that land accrue to his lord of the fee.

44. Scutage [*tax on knights' fees, paid chiefly in lieu of military service*] is to be taken henceforth as it used to be taken in the time of King Henry our grandfather.

45. All those customs aforesaid indeed and the liberties which we have granted to be held in our kingdom, in so far as it appertains to us in respect of our own people, shall <similarly> be observed by all in our kingdom, both clergy and laity, in so far as it appertains to them in respect of their own people;

46. Saving to the archbishops, bishops, abbots, priors, Templars, Hospitallers, earls, barons and all other persons, both ecclesiastical and secular, the liberties and free customs which they have formerly had.

47. We have also decreed by the common counsel of our whole kingdom that all the unlicensed castles, namely those which from the beginning of the war waged between the lord J<ohn> our father and his barons of England shall have been constructed or rebuilt, are to be at once demolished.

But because we have not yet obtained a seal, we have caused this <present charter> [*blank space left for the charter's name*] with the seals of the lord legate aforesaid and of the earl W<illiam> Marshal, guardian of us and of our kingdom, so to be sealed.

TRANSCRIPTION

MAGNA CARTA

[1217]

(Oxford, Bodleian Library, MS. Ch. Glouc. 8)

Note. No clause-numbers or paragraph divisions are present in the original. The forty-seven clause-numbers introduced into the 1217 charter by William Blackstone in his edition of 1759 (as opposed to his sixty-three clauses for the 1215 version and thirty-seven for 1225) are here printed at the starts in bold numerals. The parallel clause-numbers of 1215 and 1225, where present, are added in round brackets at the ends. Punctuation has been modernized and lightly emended, 'c/t', 'i/j' and 'u/v' forms regularized, and capital letters reduced to the starts of sentences and proper names only.

HENRICUS DEI GRATIA REX ANGLIE, DOMINUS HIBERNIE, dux Normannie, Acquitanie, et comes Andegavie, archiepiscopis, episcopis, abbatibus, prioribus, comitibus, baronibus, vicecomitibus, prepositis, ministris et omnibus baillivis et fidelibus suis presentem cartam inspecturis, salutem. Sciatis quod intuitu dei et pro salute anime nostre et animarum antecessorum et successorum nostrorum ad exaltationem sancte ecclesie et emendationem regni nostri concessimus et hac presenti carta confirmavimus pro nobis et heredibus nostris in perpetuum de consilio venerabilis patris nostri, domini Gualonis, tit<ulo> sancti Martini presbiteri cardinalis et apostolice sedis legati, domini Walteri Eborum archiepiscopi, Willelmi London<iensis> episcopi et aliorum episcoporum Anglie, et Willelmi Mariscalli comitis Pembrocie, rectoris nostri et regni nostri, et aliorum fidelium comitum et baronum nostrorum Anglie, has libertates subscriptas tenendas in regno nostro Anglie in perpetuum.

1. In primis concessimus deo et hac presenti carta nostra confirmavimus pro nobis et heredibus nostris in perpetuum, quod Anglicana ecclesia libera sit et habeat iura sua integra et libertates suas illesas. Concessimus etiam omnibus liberis hominibus regni nostri pro nobis et heredibus nostris in perpetuum omnes libertates subscriptas tenendas eis et heredibus suis de nobis et heredibus nostris. (1215, c. 1; 1225, c. 1)

2. Siquis comitum vel baronum nostrorum sive aliorum tenentium de nobis in capite per servitium militare mortuus fuerit, et cum decesserit heres eius plene etatis fuerit et relevium debeat, habeat hereditatem suam per antiquum relevium, scilicet heres vel heredes comitis de baronia comitis integra per centum libras, heres vel heredes baronis de baronia integra per centum libras, heres vel heredes militis de feodo militis integro per centum solidos ad plus, et qui minus debuerit minus det secundum antiquam consuetudinem feodorum. (1215, c. 2; 1225, c. 2)

3. Si autem heres alicuius talium fuerit infra etatem, dominus eius non habeat custodiam eius nec terre sue antequam homagium eius ceperit, et postquam talis heres fuerit in custodia cum ad etatem pervenerit scilicet viginti et unius anni habeat hereditatem suam sine relevio et sine fine, ita tamen quod si ipse <dum> infra etatem fuerit, fiat miles, nichilominus terra remaneat in custodia dominorum suorum usque ad terminum predictum. (1215, c. 3; 1225, c. 3)

4. Custos terre huiusmodi heredis qui infra etatem fuerit non capiat de terra heredis nisi rationabiles exitus et rationabiles consuetudines et rationabilia servitia et hoc sine destructione et vasto hominum vel rerum. Et si nos commiserimus custodiam alicuius alicuius talis terre vicecomiti vel alicui alii qui de exitibus terre illius nobis debeat respondere, et ille destructionem de custodia fecerit vel vastum, nos ab illo capiemus emendam, et terra committatur duobus legalibus et discretis hominibus de feodo illo qui de exitibus nobis respondeant, vel ei cui eos assignaverimus. Et si dederimus vel vendiderimus alicui custodiam alicuius talis terre et ille destructionem inde fecerit vel vastum, amittat ipsam custodiam, et tradatur duobus legalibus et discretis hominibus de feodo illo qui similiter nobis respondeant sicut predictum est. (1215, c. 4; 1225, c. 4)

5. Custos autem quamdiu custodiam terre habuerit, sustentet domos, parcos, vivarios, stagna, molendina et cetera ad terram illam pertinentia, de exitibus terre eiusdem, et reddat heredi cum ad plenam etatem pervenerit terram suam totam instauratam, de carucis et omnibus aliis rebus ad minus secundum quod illam recepit. Hec omnia observentur de custodiis archiepiscopatuum, episcopatuum, abbatiarum, prioratuum, ecclesiarum et dignitatum vacantium que ad nos pertinent, excepto quod custodie huiusmodi vendi non debent. (1215, c. 5; 1225, c. 5)

6. Heredes maritentur absque disparagatione. (1215, c. 6; 1225, c. 6)

7. Vidua post mortem mariti sui statim et sine difficultate aliqua habeat maritagium suum et hereditatem suam, nec aliquid det pro dote sua, et pro maritagio suo vel hereditate sua quam

hereditatem maritus suus et ipsa tenuerint die obitus ipsius mariti, et maneat in capitali mesuagio mariti sui per XL dies post obitum ipsius mariti sui, infra quos assignetur ei dos sua, nisi prius fuerit ei assignata, vel nisi domus illa sit castrum, et si de castro recesserit, statim provideatur ei domus competens in qua possit honeste morari, quo usque dos sua ei assignetur secundum quod predictum est. Et habeat rationabile estuverium suum interim de communi. Assignetur autem ei pro dote sua tertia pars totius terre mariti sui que sua fuit in vita sua nisi de minori dotata fuerit ad ostium ecclesie. (1215, c. 7; 1225, c. 7[a])

8. Nulla vidua distringatur ad se maritand<am> [*or* maritand<um>] dum voluerit vivere sine marito, ita tamen, quod securitatem faciat quod se non maritabit sine assensu nostro si de nobis tenuerit vel sine assensu domini sui si de alio tenuerit. (1215, c. 8; 1225, c. 7[b])

9. Nos vero vel baillivi nostri non saisiemus terram aliquam nec redditum pro debito aliquo quamdiu catalla debitoris presentia sufficiunt ad debitum reddendum, et ipse debitor paratus sit inde satisfacere, nec plegii ipsius debitoris distringantur quamdiu ipse capitalis debitor sufficiat ad solutionem debiti. Et si capitalis debitor defecerit in solutione debiti non habens unde reddat aut reddere nolit cum possit, plegii respondeant pro debito, et si voluerint, habeant terras et redditus debitoris quousque sit eis satisfactum de debito, quod ante pro eo solverint, nisi capitalis debitor monstraverit se inde esse quietum versus eosdem plegios. (1215, c. 9; 1225, c. 8)

10. Civitas London<ie> habeat omnes antiquas libertates et liberas consuetudines suas. Preterea volumus et concedimus quod omnes alie civitates et burgi, et ville, et barones de Quinque Portibus et omnes portus habeant omnes libertates et liberas consuetudines suas. (1215, c. 13; 1225, c. 9)

11. Nullus distringatur ad faciendum maius servitium de feodo militis nec de alio libero tenemento quam inde debetur. (1215, c. 16; 1225, c. 10)

12. Communia placita non sequantur curiam nostram, sed teneantur in aliquo loco certo. (1215, c. 17; 1225, c. 11)

13. Recognitiones de nova dissaisina <et> de morte antecessoris non capiantur nisi in suis comitatibus et hoc modo. Nos vel si extra regnum fuerimus capitalis iusticiarius noster mittemus iusticiarios per unumquemque comitatum semel in anno qui cum militibus comitatuum capiant in comitatibus assisas predictas. (1215, c. 18; 1225, c. 12[a])

14. Et ea que in illo adventu suo in comitatu per iusticiarios predictos ad dictas assisas capiendas missos terminari non possunt, per eosdem terminentur alibi in itinere suo, et ea que per eosdem propter difficultatem aliquorum articulorum terminari non possunt, referantur ad iusticiarios nostros de banco et ibi terminentur. (1215, c. 19; 1225, c. 12[b])

15. Assise de ultima presentatione semper capiantur coram iusticiariis de banco, et ibi terminentur. (1225, c. 13)

16. Liber homo non amercietur pro parvo delicto nisi secundum modum ipsius delicti, et pro magno delicto secundum magnitudinem delicti, salvo contenemento suo, et mercator eodem modo, salva mercandisa sua, et villanus alterius quam noster eodem modo amercietur salvo Wainagio suo si inciderit in misericordiam nostram, et nulla predictarum misericordiarum ponatur nisi per sacramenta proborum et legalium hominum de visneto. (1215, c. 20; 1225, c. 14[a])

17. Comites et barones non amercientur nisi per pares suos et non nisi secundum modum delicti. (1215, c. 21; 1225, c. 14[b])

18. Nulla ecclesiastica persona amercietur secundum quantitatem beneficii sui ecclesiastici, sed secundum laicum tenementum suum, et secundum quantitatem delicti. (1215, c. 22; 1225, c. 14[c])

19. Nec villa nec homo distringatur facere pontes ad riparias, nisi qui ab antiquo et de iure facere debet. (1215, c. 23; 1225, c. 15)

20. Nulla riparia de cetero defendatur, nisi ille que fuerunt in defenso tempore Henrici regis avi nostri per eadem loca et eosdem terminos sicut esse consueverunt tempore suo. (1225, c. 16)

21. Nullus vicecomes, constabularius, coronatores vel alii baillivi nostri teneant placita corone nostre. (1215, c. 24; 1225, c. 17)

22. Si aliquis tenens de nobis laicum feodum moriatur et vicecomes vel baillivus noster ostendat literas nostras patentes de summonitione nostra de debito quod defunctus nobis debuit, liceat vicecomiti vel baillivo nostro attachiare et inbreviare catalla defuncti inventa in laico feodo ad valentiam illius debiti per visum legalium hominum. Ita tamen, quod nichil inde amoveatur donec persolvatur nobis debitum quod clarum fuerit, et residuum relinquatur executoribus ad faciendum testamentum defuncti. Et si nichil nobis debeatur ab ipso, omnia catalla cedant defuncto, salvis uxori ipsius rationabilibus partibus suis. (1215, c. 26; 1225, c. 18)

23. Nullus constabularius vel baillivus eius capiat blada aut alia catalla alicuius qui non sit de villa ubi castrum situm est, nisi statim inde reddat denarios, aut respectum inde habere possit de voluntate venditoris. Si autem de villa ipsa fuerit infra XL dies pretium reddat. (1215, c. 28; 1225, c. 19)

24. Nullus constabularius distringat aliquem militem ad dandum denarios pro custodia castri si ipse eam facere voluerit in propria persona sua vel per alium probum hominem si ipse eam facere non possit propter rationabilem causam. Et si nos duxerimus eum vel miserimus in exercitum, erit quietus de custodia secundum quantitatem temporis quo per nos fuerit in exercitu, de feodo pro quo fecit servitium in exercitu. (1215, c. 29; 1225, c. 20)

25. Nullus vicecomes vel baillivus noster vel alius capiat equos vel carettas alicuius pro cariagio faciendo, nisi reddat liberationem antiquitus statutam, scilicet pro caretta ad duos equos decem denarios per diem, et pro caretta ad tres equos quatuordecim denarios per diem. (1215, c. 30; 1225, c. 21[a])

26. Nulla caretta dominica alicuius ecclesiastice persone vel militis vel alicuius domine capiatur per baillivos predictos. (1225, c. 21[b])

27. Nec nos nec baillivi nostri nec alii capiemus alienum boscum ad castra vel alia agenda nostra, nisi per voluntatem illius cuius boscus ille fuerit. (1215, c. 31; 1225, c. 21[c])

28. Nos non tenebimus terras eorum qui convicti fuerunt de felonia nisi per unum annum et unum diem, et tunc reddantur terre dominis feodorum. (1215, c. 32; 1225, c. 22)

29. Omnes kidelli de cetero deponantur penitus per Tamisiam, vel Medewaiam, et per totam Angliam nisi per costeram maris. (1215, c. 33; 1225, c. 23)

30. Breve quod vocatur 'precipe' de cetero non fiat alicui de aliquo tenemento, unde liber homo perdat curiam suam. (1215, c. 34; 1225, c. 24)

31. Una mensura vini sit per totum regnum nostrum, et una mensura cervisie, et una mensura bladi, scilicet quarterium London<ie>, et una latitudo pannorum tinctorum, et russetorum, et haubergetorum, scilicet due ulne infra listas. De ponderibus vero sit ut de mensuris. (1215, c. 35; 1225, c. 25)

32. Nichil detur de cetero pro brevi inquisitionis ab eo qui inquisitionem petit de vita vel membris, sed gratis concedatur et non negetur. (1215, c. 36; 1225, c. 26)

33. Si aliquis teneat de nobis per feodifirmam vel soccagium vel per burgagium, et de alio teneat terram per servitium militare, nos non habebimus custodiam heredis nec terre sue que est de feodo alterius occasione illius feodifirme vel soccagii vel burgagii. Nec habebimus custodiam illius feodifirme vel soccagii vel burgagii, nisi ipsa feodifirma debeat servitium militare. Nos non habebimus custodiam heredis vel terre alicuius quam tenet de alio per servitium militare, occasione alicuius parve sergentarie quam tenet de nobis per servitium reddendi cultellos vel sagittas vel huiusmodi. (1215, c. 37; 1225, c. 27)

34. Nullus baillivus ponat de cetero aliquem ad legem manifestam nec ad iuramentum simplici loquela sua, sine testibus fidelibus ad hoc inductis. (1215, c. 38; 1225, c. 28)

35. Nullus liber homo capiatur vel imprisonetur aut dissaisietur de libero tenemento suo vel libertatibus vel liberis consuetudinibus suis, aut utlagetur aut exuletur aut aliquo alio modo destruatur, nec super eum ibimus, nec super eum mittemus, nisi per legale iudicium parium suorum vel per legem terre. (1215, c. 39; 1225, c. 29[a])

36. Nulli vendemus, nulli negabimus aut differemus rectum aut iustitiam. (1215, c. 40; 1225, c. 29[b])

37. Omnes mercatores, nisi publice antea prohibiti fuerint, habeant salvum et securum conductum exire de Anglia, et venire in Angliam, et morari, et ire per Angliam, tam per terram quam per aquam ad emendendum [*for* emendum] vel vendendum, sine omnibus toltis malis, per antiquas et rectas consuetudines preterquam in tempore guerre. Et si sint de terra contra nos guerriva, et si tales inveniantur in terra nostra in principio guerre, attachientur sine dampno corporum vel rerum, donec sciatur a nobis vel a capitali iusticiario nostro quomodo mercatores terre nostre tractentur qui tunc inveniantur in terra contra nos guerriva. Et si nostri salvi sint ibi, alii salvi sint in terra nostra. (1215, c. 41; 1225, c. 30)

38. Siquis tenuerit de aliqua excaeta sicut de honore Walingford', Bolon', Notingeham', Lancastr', vel de aliis escaetis que sunt in manu nostra, et sint baronie, et obierit, heres eius non det aliud relevium nec faciet nobis aliud servitium quam faceret baroni si illa esset in manu baronis et nos eodem modo eam tenebimus quo baro eam tenuit. Nec nos occasione talis baronie vel excaete habebimus aliquam excaetam vel custodiam aliquorum hominum nostrorum nisi alibi tenuerit de nobis in capite ille qui tenuit baroniam vel excaetam. (1215, c. 43; 1225, c. 31)

39. Nullus liber homo de cetero det amplius alicui vel vendat de terra sua quam ut de residuo terre sue possit sufficienter fieri domino feodi servitium ei debitum quod pertinet ad feodum illud. (1225, c. 32)

40. Omnes patroni abbatiarum qui habent cartas regum Anglie, de advocatione, vel antiquam tenuram vel possessionem habeant earum custodiam cum vacaverint sicut habere debent et sicut supra declaratum est. (1215, c. 46; 1225, c. 33)

41. Nullus capiatur vel imprisonetur propter appellum femine de morte alterius quam viri sui. (1215, c. 54; 1225, c. 34)

42. Nullus comitatus de cetero teneatur nisi de mense in mensem, et ubi maior terminus esse solebat maior sit. Nec aliquis vicecomes vel baillivus suus faciat turnum suum per hundredum nisi bis in anno, et non nisi in loco debito et consueto, videlicet semel post Pascha, et iterum post festum sancti Michaelis. Et visus de franco plegio tunc fiat ad illum terminum sancti Michaelis, sine occasione, ita scilicet quod quilibet habeat libertates suas quas habuit et habere consuevit tempore Henrici regis avi nostri, vel quas postea perquisivit. Fiat autem visus de franco plegio sic videlicet quod pax nostra teneatur et quod tethinga integra sit sicut esse consuevit, et quod vicecomes non querat occasiones et quod contentus sit de eo quod vicecomes habere consuevit de visu suo faciendo tempore Henrici regis avi nostri. (1225, c. 35)

43. Non liceat alicui de cetero dare terram suam alicui domui religiose ita quod illam resumat tenendam de eadem domo. Nec liceat alicui domui religiose terram alicuius sic accipere quod tradat eam illi a quo eam receperit tenendam. Siquis autem de cetero terram suam alicui domui religiose sic dederit, et super hoc convincatur donum suum penitus cassetur et terra illa domino suo illius feodi incurratur. (1225, c. 36)

44. Scutagium capiatur de cetero sicut capi consuevit tempore Henrici regis avi nostri. (1225, c. 37[a])

45. Omnes autem istas consuetudines predictas et libertates quas concessimus in regno nostro tenendas quantum ad nos pertinet erga nostros, omnes de regno nostro, tam clerici quam laici, observent quantum ad se pertinet erga suos; (1215, c. 60; 1225, c. 37[c])

46. salvis archiepiscopis, episcopis, abbatibus, prioribus, templariis, hospitalariis, comitibus, baronibus, et omnibus aliis tam ecclesiasticis personis quam secularibus, libertatibus et liberis consuetudinibus quas prius habuerunt. (1225, c. 37[b])

47. Statuimus etiam de communi consilio totius regni nostri quod omnia castra adulterina videlicet ea que a principio guerre mote inter dominum J<ohannem> patrem nostrum et barones suos Anglie constructa fuerint vel reedificata, statim diruantur.

Quia vero nondum habuimus sigillum hanc [*blank space*] <presentem cartam> sigillis domini legati predicti et comitis W<illelmi> Mariscalli rectoris et regni nostri fecimus sigillari.